Celebrate the Mystery

Celebrate the Mystery

A Mother's Journey of Awakening Through Cancer

Suzanne Elaine Lindemer

edited and arranged by
Eric Brian Lindemer

TABLE OF CONTENTS

Foreword

It is with great pleasure that I present this collection of excerpts from my mother's journal, in which she explored her experiences of living with cancer and the challenges, triumphs, insights, and growth that occurred for her along the way. Whether you are facing an illness, care about someone who is, work in healthcare or healing, or are interested in personal and spiritual growth, I feel that something in my mother's journal will speak to you.

When Mom was diagnosed with terminal pancreatic cancer she was given less than a year to live. Quite remarkably, she survived almost four. In addition to chemotherapy and radiation, she turned to journaling, meditation, visualization, music therapy, personal growth, and spiritual expansion in her plan to fight cancer and embrace life. With the hope that her reflections might be of benefit to others, she was working towards publishing her journal until shortly before her passing in October of 1990.

In preparing this collection, I assumed I would keep the entries I selected in chronological order as she had them in her journal. However, after pouring over them multiple times, I noticed distinct themes emerging, and decided to use these themes as chapter titles with which to organize the entries. With this arrangement, readers have the option of turning to a particular chapter that appeals to them at any given time.

I have included my mother's own heartfelt introduction, which she wrote many years ago.

It's an honor to share my mother's journal with you.

Eric Brian Lindemer
January 11, 2015

Introduction

When I am not physically maneuvering a couch to the far end of the room or coaxing a library table into a spot under the windows, I'm likely to be mentally mapping plans for the next time we rearrange the room. Actually, it's my husband who does most of the moving while I suggest where to try things next. If not bursting with enthusiasm for the job, he's usually willing enough to help, although this congenial willingness begins to dim by the time he's moved the couch to the third "perfect spot." It's about then that he's apt to take pleasure in citing the archaic Kentucky law prohibiting wives from rearranging furniture without their husband's permission.

Some arrangements are seasonal; certainly prime space must be made for the Christmas tree. But more often my motivation comes from the fun of trying something new and the challenge of waking up our senses. Once a pattern becomes too familiar it seems we barely see it anymore, and we certainly stop noticing the details.

Rearrangements of furniture can change the whole feel of a room. Moving a drawing or watercolor to a different wall enables us to both literally and figuratively see it in a new light.

In my journal I write about rearranging furniture. I also write about rearranging my own interior.

By the time I learned I had cancer, changes in my body had already begun. With treatment there would be more changes. Some I authorized; some just happened. Not as suddenly, but very markedly and with conscious awareness, I began to rearrange other parts of myself. This rearrangement of my physical, mental, emotional and spiritual interior is the essence of this journal.

It begins a few days after I was given a diagnosis of terminal pancreatic cancer in December 1986.

While I was still in the hospital, attempting to absorb the enormity of the diagnosis, a friend brought me a book of blank pages, handsomely bound in deep rose fabric with birds ascending its cover. The birds are cranes, I think, symbol of peace and healing. I was hesitant at first to mar its pristine beauty with the dark feelings I was experiencing, so I limited my writing to fragments scrawled in the notebook I used for medical questions, all the while keeping an eye on her appealing gift.

As periods of consciousness increased between sleep and medication, I began to realize how essential it was for me to begin to consciously allow full expression to all dimensions of my pain: physical, mental, emotional, and spiritual. My friend knew that writing would be a way for me to do it. Before long I did initiate the expectant pages of the book, crossing out, rewriting, scribbling in the margins with abandon, no longer constrained by its virginal state. Five volumes later I am still at it.

Journal writing is intensely personal. Initially I had no intention of sharing what I was writing. I found, however, that I was moving into a period of tremendous growth and I did begin to share my writing. As I did so I discovered that it contains a universality of human experience that speaks to readers who are not involved with cancer, as well as those who are.

My task then became to not allow my writing to be influenced by the thought of others reading it, or by any need I might feel to please them or to present myself in favorable light. A conscious exception to this is the fact that I am less descriptive about some of my relationships than I would be if I were writing in a diary with lock and key. Even so I reveal myself in ways I would not ordinarily do. I'm willing to risk the exposure, knowing my experience is sometimes meaningful to others.

I have edited these published entries sparingly in an attempt to not dilute the impact of their frank, uncensored immediacy. Many of the entries are spontaneous. Others are more reflective with finer crafting. One reader has called them snapshots which capture changing events and moods.

I want to share my experience that we can deal with cancer on many levels. Meditation, imaging, psychotherapy, support groups and spiritual growth can work with the traditional protocols of surgery, chemotherapy and radiation.

I want to share my experience that the very grimness of a prognosis can help one break through years-old layers of resistance to allow an opening to multiple levels of growth. A June 5, 1987, journal entry:

> I would gladly
> Give back the cancer if
> I could, but
> I want to
> Keep all it
> Has taught me.

I want to share my experience that honestly confronting the prospect of premature death is propelling me into living more fully, more openly and more consciously than I ever thought possible.

It would please me if my experience might help others find ways to nourish their own growth, to rearrange their own space. It is in this spirit that I share my journal.

Suzanne Lindemer
July 18, 1990

1

Life Forever Changed

They gathered

The doctor with the
Horrible abstract of
His news in a folder

The husband at the
Foot of the bed at the
Foot of the patient where
He could touch and see her

Two children
Seated to the left
Each one straining to
Reach and caress a
Hand or an arm

We knew what it would be

The patient could
Tell from the
Stricken
Controlled
Faces of the family
Five days earlier when
She began to
Surface from anesthesia

The family knew how
Certain the doctor was of his
Feared diagnosis but
Waited with him for the
Final biopsy to
Confirm it

The shock was
Initially
Not so much in the
Content but in the
Delivery
How gracefully
Elegantly yet without
Artifice
He relayed his
Lethal sentence

Then the
Horribleness of
"nothing can be done" the
Knowledge that
Life would pulsate through this
Body for only a matter of
Weeks or
Months or perhaps a
Year began to
Penetrate the
Chill marrow of being

Through the
Despair the
Terror the
Overwhelming sadness
It was hard to buy his
Contention that how much better
It is to know of
Impending death to
Know
Love and
Cherish

For two days
I could tolerate
Seeing very few people

My escape was in sleep

Each awakening
Jolted me back to
Reality and the
Overwhelming
Sadness of my
Dream:

Husband and children
Play in the yard as
I watch from
Upstairs window

Unable to participate

No longer a part of them

Through the days of
Sleep and tears my
Body becomes super sensitive

Injections bring actual
Cries of agony

Tube from nose to stomach
Continues its painful placement

As veins fall
Repeated stabs must find
New locations for IVs

Despair
Pain
Abandonment prevail

Why am I trying to
Get better just to
Go home and
Get sick and die

Home again

It's what I wanted but
Now that I'm here it's both
Comforting and cruel

The old and familiar
Delight my eye
Sleeping next to my husband
Means more than it ever has but

Knowing I'm going to
Leave all this soon

Even the pictures on the wall

More
Those who
Dwell within

Makes me sad
Brings death even
Closer into view

Notes
Calls
Visits from
Friends repeat the question I ask:
Why?

Their sadness
Anger
Frustration almost
Surpasses my own

I cry in
Response to their
Caring

Writing Christmas cards
Is like telling 56
Friends and Family
Good-bye

I managed to sing
Most of "Silent Night"
No tears escaped as
We lit our candles and the
Magical warmth of
Christmas Eve descended

It was good to be in
Church and with
People
Good to feel the
Warm hugs and
Bright greetings and to

Know that when
I die the
Protective arms of these
Caring people will
Enclose my family and
Let them grieve and
Offer them love

Damn it!
I was looking forward to being a
Funny old lady with
You and a
Few others

We would have a
Whale of a good time with
Age our excuse for
Being outspoken

We would have much to
Remember together
Would pride ourselves on
Remaining current

You and the others
Will do it just
Fine without me but
I'll miss you

I'm both
Angry and
Sad that
I'm going to
Miss so much

Not just their
Big events
Graduations
Jobs
Weddings
Grandchildren but the

Occasional
Note in the mail
The more often
Talks on the phone about
What's happening now

I'm sorry not to be there to
Listen to their
Struggles
Rejoice in their
Triumphs and

Just to not
Know them
Any more

I wonder
Where does the
Difference
Lie between
Realistic
Acceptance and
Giving up

2

Hospitals, Doctors, and Treatment

It's not that I don't
Appreciate their
Concern and the
Fact that they
Want to help
Somehow

Each one knows a
Cousin of a
Sister-in-law who
Has the same thing and his
Doctor has a
Far different approach

I have been asked if I
Need additional spiritual help
I've been advised to
   adopt a macrobiotic diet
Why does my doctor not
   give me chemotherapy
Do I know about the
   cancer center in
   Ohio
   Texas
   New York

Another is much too eager
   to graphically
Describe the stages his
   loved one went through
Do I know how much
   difference a support
   group can make

Now the information
   we requested from the
National Cancer Institute
   has arrived and put
Me into a further
   emotional tailspin

Exhausted
Confused
Tears spent
I slouch in the chair

Information
Advice still
Flow in
Much from
People and sources
I respect but
They are contradictory
Unproven
Confusing
How do I choose?
What approach do I embrace?

One of the
First conflicts
I must resolve
Is to no longer be
Concerned over what
"Others will think" if I
Do one thing and
Don't do others
What worked for them
May not be best for me

I look for
Strength
Guidance
Courage to
Find the way

Radiation makes such
    an urgent sound
A rasping wail that
    rises and falls
The fluctuations
    sound convincing
I really think it can shoot
    deadly rays through me

I relax into myself
Allow love and peace to
Soften me and
Trust the rays to
Find their mark

Two baskets
One bag

Books
Journals
Letters
Music
Notebooks
Quotes

Follow me from
Bedroom to
Couch to
Studio to
Hospital

I need them
Plunked around me to
Know what I need
Is there

Always
Mozart
Must be
There

Another round of
Radiation ended!
I feel like a
Fifth grader on
Summer vacation

The destruction of blood cells
White red and platelets
Seems an acceptable
Risk with chemotherapy
A kind of justifiable homicide

They are no less essential to
Life than my other
Threatened parts yet
They seem less personal
More abstract and
They do regenerate with
Transfusions and a
Rest from chemo

Knowing I am authorizing the
Destruction of a certain organ
Seems much more personal and
Intimate more like
Premeditated murder

Maybe it's partly numbers
There are so many blood cells
Rather anonymously
Flowing through my body
Doing many jobs efficiently
They are rather taken for granted

A kidney has a particular
Mass shape location
It shows up clearly in
Transparent overlays of
Body parts in the encyclopedia

So does the pancreas
I hope it appreciates
All the sacrifices the
Rest of the body is making for it

I feel vulnerable
My white blood count is
Down

It feels like a
Protective coating has been
Removed

I stand exposed
Subject to every
Infection about me

Dangerous gaps exist where
The circled wagons are
Spread too thin

Another
Stay of execution
Is how it feels

My platelets and
White count are
Too low for chemo

So it's wait
Another week
Second time in a row

I absorb the
Beauty of
October

Touch the chill
See the freshness
Inhale the colors

Wade in the
Gift of these
Golden days

Thankful to
Be a part of
Them

Rather than an
Observer from
6-East

Trailing my chemo pump to
Corridor windows to
View autumn

I turned off the
Artificiality of
Air-conditioning
Opened the
Window to the
Reality of
Wind and sun

Turned up the
Volume on the
Radio so
Petrushka
Swelled
Around me the
Expansiveness of the
Stravinsky score in
Fair consort with
Billowing sky

Strident
Angular Passages
Heralded by
Insistent trumpet
Became a
Preamble to the
Darkening
Sky and
Stabs of
Lightening
Ahead

The rain
When it came
Obliterated sight
I welcomed the
Drenching as I
Dashed from the
Pharmacy
Delighted to be
Amid the elements
Before tomorrow's
Cocooning on the
Oncology floor

It's time to gather
Books music courage

Move into 6-East for
Another round of chemo

Bring all of me that
I can to the experience

Take all that I can
From it

New peace
Acceptance
Energy

Unite in the hospital

Warmth of
Caring contacts
Welcomes me

Nice things
Have happened today
Warm connections
Have been made
Immediate real words
Have been said

When I am
Isolated in a
Hospital room
I think my
Main connection is to
My chemo pump but
Today everything
Changed that

Tom down the hall
Left today and brought me his
Flowers and news of seeking a
Bone marrow transplant now that
His leukemia is in remission

He's a fourth-year medical student
We spoke about how his illness will
Affect his compassion as a doctor

His large grin
In his
Thin face
Peered out from
Under his
Andy's Cookies red hat that
Covers his hair loss

As anxious as he was to
Leave he found it hard to
Unplug the connections here

Graduate nursing
Student friend
Elizabeth who is
Doing clinicals at
Another hospital
Came for an extended
Afternoon stay and
Very real sharing
She brought me a
Stephen Levine
Meditation tape on pain
I gave her a copy of my writing

We spoke of
Religion Yoga Self-discovery
Her work with
Cancer patients and
Plans for leading them on an
Outward Bound excursion

Connections for this moment
Connections for the future
Welcome entanglements
Connections in spirit
Abound

Lori Patti and Lois
Came in often
Today to talk
Busy nurses and
Supervisor taking
Time to minister to
More than the body

Their presence and
Interest buoyed me
Their sharing
Their lives and
Concerns with me
Felt so vital genuine
Like I was a real
Member of society
More than just a
Cancer patient in their
Care on the
Oncology floor

Dr. N. and I
While she thumped my back
Marveled that Beethoven
Could have composed his
Magnificent Ninth
While deaf!

If she weren't so young
You might think she is a
Holdover from the
Third Reich
Eager to add another
Victim to her
Medical experiments

Her pale eyes are
Flat and cold
Her mouth unusually neutral
It doesn't frown and
It certainly doesn't smile but
Consciously betrays
No emotion

She doesn't like
Patients who
Ask questions
Prod for details
Take her time
Write things down

She would prefer a
Patient who would
Unquestioningly put herself in
Madame Doctor's hands and
Become another
Decimal point in the
Data of her
Clinical trial

One cried with me the
Day after my diagnosis

One gives unstintingly of his time
Is not afraid to deal with dying and
Assures me he will be there
Is there now to talk with

One spreads sunshine with his smile
Assures me he'll always
Tell me the truth
The problem is I need to
Ask the right questions

One gives me information and
Says body mind spirit soul
Well at least body and mind interact
Just nobody can prove it yet
He smiles not with
Amusement but with
Pleasure when I
Describe my imaging

Family physician
Surgeon
Oncologist
Radiologist oncologist
Doctors with human parts among their
Scientific credentials with
Time and awareness to say
"I like your earrings"

What I hear is
"I see you as a person"

Leucovorin
You are borin'

You cause sores on my gum
In my throat on my tongue
All down my esophagus
Yet more preposterous
Than the sores interior
Are those posterior!

A glass of wine
Would sure be fine

A chilled Moselle
Would go down well

But with this chemo
I get no vino

It's so hard to remember
So hard to remember
So difficult to believe that
I will get over the
Rottenness of the first day
Home after chemo

I try to make myself
Listen and
Remember I always
Feel this way but
Each time it
Seems as never before

But then
Finally
Comes that precious glint of hope
A minute pulse of feeling good that
Means in a few hours or a day the
Curtain will pull back and
I'll feel a part of life again

It's a balance between
Curling into a ball to
Wait it out so I can survive and
Taking sample forages to
Set rhythms in motion again

Voyage too soon and
Digestive rhythms
Hurry me back to port
Linger too long and
More in missed than need be

Grey
Cold
Rain

Encourages a
Day of

Rest
Recovery
Refilling

The wave of
Realization that
My treatment is
Working begins to
Flow into my
Consciousness
I become
Aware of a
Gentle
Certainty that
Rests
Comfortably
Within me
A quiet elation
Fills my being

Lucy wasn't
Supposed to die

Lucy was
Doing better

I know
Her father told me so

I know
I could hear her cough less

I know
Her husband and daughter smiled

I know
Her mother refreshed her with a sponge bath

I left on Friday
She died on Sunday

I know
Tonight's paper told me so

She called today
After three years of remission
She has a recurrence of
Breast cancer

She is calm
Ready to deal with the present
After an extra year of life
No one thought she would have

She calls this event
"Part of the cost of living"
And is not bitter

"I don't feel despair
I've learned to live vigorously"
She says and
Heads off for surgery
Actively investigating
Her options for the
Future

She gives me strength

It's Scary
Understandably so

He can feel more
He wants to order
Another scan
Right away

I don't want
It to grow
I want to keep
Keeping it at
Bay with
Chemo and
Imaging

I want time to
Learn to
Let more
Healing harmony
Grow inside me
Rampant as a
Malignancy

Imagination

Isn't that a
Marvelous word for a
Doctor to use in
Explaining what is
Necessary beside
Textbook facts in
Treating patients

He used many other
Words in this
Caring conversation

Words that allowed his
Humanness to be
Exposed
Good words but more
Predictable words

Imagination
Had the greatest
Impact
It was not a word I
Expected

Coming back to the
Oncology floor is
Coming back to
Caring
Sharing
Encouragement
Accepting

Strong concerns
Strong connections
Find voice with
Little preamble.
Short shrift is
Given to the weather.

It's a place where
Reality, tempered with
Compassion,
Can bloom,
Free from our usual need to
Cushion feelings,
Protect one another,
Avoid real feelings.

We all know what
We're dealing with so
Let's get on with it.

I settle into
Round 11

Tempering
Positive action with
Passive allowing acceptance

I allow my
Will my ego to
Float up and be
Absorbed supported carried by
Spiritual awareness

A letting go that
Allows me to
Become a part of
Something more than
This hospital room
This treatment
This me

Blood had been drawn
Weight and height questions done
While we wait for chemo to begin
We escape to the brisk day
Seek the sun and bright leaves
Know what it means to be free
Focused on the moment

We fairly dance as we spot
Magnificent leaves in
Never-before-seen
Colors and combinations
Fill our pockets with
Their brilliance
Share the miracle of their being

In a burst of pure inspiration
We tape them to the window in a
Configuration of gusty propulsion
Across the pane with
Careful attention given to the
Crucial placement of the last few

The light streaming in
Makes them translucent
Infusing them with life
Doctors patients nurses
Come to marvel with us at
Mother Nature on the sixth floor

Now this hospital
Responds when it can

I talked to the clinical
Specialist about Cousins* and
Laughter
Next morning at ten we had
Candid Camera tapes for
Patients families staff

The student nurses
Learned a lot I think
They could see wonderful fun
Individual release and
Collective courage

In response to my
Need to know more about
How blood cells look
(For my imaging)
Graduate student friend
Brought hematology atlas
Doctor suggested yet
Another volume
Student nurse arranged a
Visit to the lab where
They had a lovely slide of
Red cells white cells and
Platelets all in focus
Just waiting for us!

People care!
A hospital can be lots
More than tests and
Needles and medicine

*Norman Cousins, pioneer of laughter therapy (editor's note)

We all heard it
Every patient on the floor
All through the night

The eventuality
We all fear the
Most

Lack of control of
Body mind
Spirit

We were sorry for him
But more fearful for
Selves

His calling out
His pain
His delirium from morphine

Nurses embarrassed
They couldn't
Control his needs

The next morning he sits
Unshaven hollow-eyed
On the side of his bed

I'm sorry
I didn't
Go to him

The floor is somber
Many very ill patients
Dear Cathy in increasing pain
Doors and faces are closed
I don't know how to
Help them nor
Me

We escape on the
Elevator to floor three
Cribs of newborns
Light our faces
Rekindle joy and hope

Support Group

The strength
The understanding that
Inherently bubbles among us
The comfort
The Vitality of
Being with those who
Really know
What it's like
Combine in spirit
Rise above us to
Form a good cloud which
Sprinkles gentle rain
(Or rains gentle sprinkles) of
Hope and caring
Over us all

He was tired when
He came in at 6:15
Conceded he needed to sit down

He told me
(He thought I knew)
She died

He wanted to talk about it
See how it impacted me
Remind me we are
Two different people

Wanted to bring it
Out in the open
Not hide from it

He told me how
Profoundly she affected him
How he respected her intelligence
How difficult it was to help her

What anger he holds toward the
Doctor whom he feels gave her
Misleading counsel

As I reflect on it
Several hours hence
I think he was saying
"I want you to know
I can be there for you"

I must tell him
I believe that

He parts with
"I'm not on call
This weekend but
Call me at home if
You need me"

Large nurse Mike
Who gave me such
Tender care for two days
Brought his adorable
Baby daughter by to
See me on his day off
While on his way to a
Baby shower for the
Oncology floor clinical specialist

How nice to see him in a
Red shirt instead of his whites
How especially meaningful for
Him to share such a
Personal side of himself with me
His obviously beloved daughter
Wrapped in pink

Eight days in the hospital.

I feel like I want to go out and
Do something weird and connective,

Like gnaw bark on the tree;

Something to shock my system
Back into connection with the
Real world outside.

This is real.
This is how it tastes.
This is how it feels.
This is earth.
I am a part of it.

Rx for depression:
Fly away on a plane
Do things ordinary folk do
Leave doctors hospital
Tests and treatments behind
Move through crowds where
No one knows I have cancer
Then maybe even I can
Forget for a little while

I function as
Two different people
One does "real life" things the
Other deals with cancer

During the twenty or so
Days a month that my
Health ranges from feeling
Pretty good to extremely well
I cook clean shop
Write letters lunch with friends
Take walks make Christmas gifts
Market my note cards
Read think write work in therapy
Travel go to church plays concerts
Dinners music appreciation class and hear
"My you look wonderful"
Some days I rarely
Think of cancer

When the time comes to do
Another five days of chemo and
Endure the recovery period
I am immersed in
Cancer pain hospital
Patients doctors nurses
Families in distress
Tests new knowledge
New questions new doubts
New fears new insights
I am very much aware
I am a cancer patient
The best way for me to cope is to
Actively enter this world be an
Enthusiastic participant
Bring energy and good humor to
The days I am able
Go out to meet and be available to
Other patients and families until
My days of night come and
I retreat to lick my wounds
Search for the faith that
I will survive
Again

If cures are
Few and
Far between

I'll settle for a
Good share of
Living with cancer

Right now
Two years sounds like a
Gift from eternity

I felt so incredibly
Good for three days
I couldn't believe it

I called the pharmacist
Suspicious that one of my new
Prescriptions might be the
Real cause of my euphoria

He assured me there were no
Stimulants in any of them

It's real
This feeling
It's me

3

Making Death's Acquaintance

The first several times
I heard it in December
I thought "How nice-
They must have thought
I would be emaciated and
Green-
They are pleased to
See I am not"

Each time I hear it and
I continue to
Often
I am surprised
I've never known people to
Tell me
"You look beautiful"

I think the beauty they sense
Is the glow of the
Intensity of the
Joy of life
I feel
Ignited by an
Acquaintance with death

Now that
Death is
Impending and
No longer a
Philosophical
Abstract
Life comes into
Sharper focus

Simple acts
Take on the
Importance of
Holy Ritual

A walk with
A friend
Transcends
Time and space
Becomes a
Sparkling jewel of
Comfort and
Love

I envisioned no particular
Time of death but
I rather assumed I wouldn't
Be here this summer then
I realized I don't
Have to die then
I may but
I don't have to

For an instant the
Part of me that is more
Concerned with others
Than with myself thought
How inconvenient it will be for
Them if I am ill during the summer

It was so blatant
It made me laugh
The hell with inconvenience
It's a poor excuse for death

The books rave on about
"The Will to Live" and
Make a distinction between
Creative and
Destructive
Forces within

Has anyone considered that
Death may be the most
Creative experience going

To live is to
Win

To die is to
Lose

No
Not
So

I'm trying to get
My life together to
Find the reality of
Who I am to
Discover the
Meaning of my living

The process is
Its own reward
It's in the doing that
Meaning evolves
Dichotomies unite
Acceptance occurs

Warmth love insight
Live within the
Pain and doubt
To be open to the
Reality of them all
Transcends their
Separateness

I want to know
Them so
I can live

I want to know
Them so
I can die

Death waits in the
Wings like an
Off-stage
Voice for the cue to
Project beyond the
Footlights into the
Heart of the drama

Those who
Know the score
Await the entry

My need is to
Explore the
Depths of death to

Examine the
Hidden corners the
Frightening turns

I want to
Know
What will
Happen
Physically
Emotionally
Spiritually

It's the journey that
Interests me more than the
Destination

I like the
Relatedness of
Birth and death

The struggle
Through the tunnel
Toward the light

Seems an
Appropriate image for
Both

I wonder
Did we spend so
Much time in

The womb
Asking what
Comes next

I feel content with my
Present perception of the
Hereafter

I expect it will be
Greater and more whole than
I can ever imagine

I don't think Mother
Will greet me in her
Print dress
Dad in his suit but

I do think there will be a
Fulfilling uniting and
Connecting with all of the
Universe and a
Place just right for me

I feel that in a sense
I will know my sister who
Died when I was too
Young to remember

I feel sure that
Most parts of Paradise
Will far outshine our
Earthly concepts

The part I'm not
Sure about however is
Music

Angelic choirs could
Become a bit tedious
After a while

Perhaps we'll perceive
Harmonious tones set in motion
Through stellar vibrations

Even so I'm becoming a
Compulsive listener
Just in case

I hear now with
Greater clarity and
Must know titles and composers

When the radio
Doesn't fill my needs
I raid the record shelves

Ella Sarah Joe Williams with
Count Basie
The Three B's
The Four Seasons of Vivaldi and
Schubert's *Die Winterreise*
Fill my ears and being

I listen for now and
I listen for later
I tuck some in my soul so
I can call them forth for an
Impromptu concert among
The spheres

I think I will
Ask that my
Body be cremated

It sounds
Revolutionary because
I don't know
Anyone in our
Family who has

No
I think there was a
Story about an urn of ashes
Maybe Grandpa's sister
She was revolutionary but
Accepted
A Christian Scientist who
Lived in California and
Was divorced

A relatively quick
Immolation and
Return to dust has
Qualities of
Purification and
Release that a
Slow disintegration
Confined within
Claustrophobic space
Beneath ground
Lacks

An eventual
Scattering of my
Remains by the ocean
Would be a satisfying
Completion of the
Life cycle and a
Release of the soul for me
A return to the
Part of the earth
I loved most in life

I think about
Death, about a

Part of
Consciousness
Surviving
Bodily death.

Perhaps
Identity does not
Survive.

I imagine an
Agreeable melting of the
Ego in a
Uniting with a
Greater All,
Experiencing the
Wholeness we seek.

It makes death O.K.

Death
Becomes
Accessible

All the brave sounds
I made about Death now
Clang in my head.

Terror replaces
Romanticized concept.

Feeling of dying
Towards something
Vanishes.

Specter of
Uncertain oblivion arises, with
All I know, am, hope
Vanishing.

Museums
Put me in touch with
Ancients who have died, with
Beloved artists who have died.

Was Van Gogh's
Soul
Tormented?
In terror?

Did Egyptians of rank
Take comfort in
Carrying so much of
This life to their
Afterlife?

Many mornings ago
I sat at the
Kitchen table
Alone
After breakfast
Following the
Daring journey of a
Fearless squirrel
Navigating a
Tree-top
Thin limb
Pathway

He could
Travel so
Swiftly so
Securely because
He didn't
Consider
Falling

I must have
Considered
It for him

The message
He brought me was
Death

It was not
Frightening nor
Upsetting just
Certain

With all my
Reading
Discussing
Pondering
I thought
I had accepted the
Fact that
We all must die

Perhaps I
Had on an
Intellectual plain

Now I was
Accepting it on
Another level
Emotionally
Absorbing the
Reality

How strange that
This unknowing
Squirrel would
Bring me
Such a
Gift

One reason it is good to
Become acquainted with
Death

Is so you know
No one else can die for you

You have to do it yourself so

No one else can live for you either

It does seem that at
Death
All senses must be heightened

Mind heart soul and body
Must know one another
Intimately and

Feel their fullness
Live their freedom

My words are too cautious
Too controlled for the moment but
I don't know how to say the
Wonder of what I feel

Perhaps because I do feel it
So securely so comfortably
I don't feel the need to
Make words sound convincing

The words are simple
The meanings are rich
I turn from
Dying to
Living

I'm going to live
I don't know how long but
I'm doing it right now

I'm investing in the
Future because I know
I'm going to have one

I have the wonderful
Awesome task of deciding
What to do with my life

How delicate how sublime
How gutsy the choices can be
What ecstasy to know I can

I begin by buying a new
Typewriter and
Rearranging the furniture

I experience a
Contentment of spirit,
Peace,
Love encompassing,
Being with me.

I feel in a new place,
Renewed with spirit,
Ready to
Bring all
Forces and
Awareness
I am able,
Open to
New avenues of
Healing.

Some of this freedom
Stems from becoming
Closer to death,
Being more with it,

So now I can allow my Self to
Spring from it,
Once again
Embrace living,

Willing to
Invest in its
Demanding efforts,
Knowing many
Forces are there to help me.

Fear of flying diminishes
I feel quite invincible to
Other forms of death

There's no need to hold back
Balanchine's dictum applies
"What are you saving it for, dear?"*

Courage gained from facing
Cancer death chemo radiation Self
Spills over to color all of life in
Vivid shades

I like my new palette

* choreographer and New York City Ballet co-founder George Balanchine speaking to one
of his dancers (editor's note)

4

The Many Faces of Pain

Pain

At first it feels like
Far-off thunder
Rumbling its warning of the
Storm to come

I hope for a
Period of grace
Before the
Full fury of the
Gale erupts and
Takes its toll

Like a child with
    weak ankles on the
First day of the
    skating season
Venturing out on the
    unproven ice
So I collect my spirits and
    courage after a
Day of pain and fear and with
    tentative steps
Approach life again
    wary of the
Fragility of thin ice

I don't want to take the
   strong pills for pain yet
It would feel like giving in

Like saying it's O.K. to become
   addicted to this narcotic since
I am a terminal case anyway

I'm already addicted to writing
   I don't think I could survive the
Pain and uncertainty without it

It also reminds me that some days are glorious

My pain and tears
Cut into him
He is patient
Strong...and there

The pain and
Suffering of
A hard death
Frighten me and

Make me so
Very sorry that
He and the
Children
Will suffer

Could I but spare them that

I've been alone today
Aware of their vitality and energy
Their bodies that eat and
Move and do not hurt

I'm feeling sorry for myself
Feel shut out from their activity
Buying the tree
Shopping for shoes
Looking for presents
Going to Knoxville together
They won't be home 'til late

By then I'll be able to
Stop crying

I am taking seven medications
I wear ugly white anti-embolism hose
Painful sores line my mouth and esophagus
My stomach hurts
Every fiber is sore

I look an in-val-id
I feel in-va-lid

It's night
I hurt
I cry

Not only my
Body but
Also my
Soul

Knows the dark
Feels the pain
Cries out as it
Strains for wholeness

I don't feel
I have the energy to
Find myself
Comfort myself
Accept and
Love this
Glob who is so unwell
Physically and emotionally

Everyone knows
Too much about me
I would have been
Better off
Operating on a more even keel
Keeping more of me in
Protected
(Even as I write this
I know
It's not true
But I feel so
At the moment)

I want to
Heave my shoe
Through the
Window

I want it to
Crash
Through the
Pane (the pain?)

I want the rage
Within me to
Explode with the
Glass

My rubber-soled
(Rubber souled?)
Shoe hits
With a thud

The glass remains
Intact
Transparent
Impenetrable

The cancer remains
My force
Too weak to
Break through

What makes depression
So immensely devastating

Yet also makes
Rescue possible

Is the remembered glint of
A whole heart
Ready to risk life again

What has happened to
All the progress
I thought I had made

Why am I now
Thrown back into
This abyss of
Terror and pain

I don't know what I am afraid of.
Why am I in such pain?
Why am I afraid to
    See what is there,
    Admit what is there,
    Deal with what is there.

It feels like it will destroy me.

I should know it will set me free.

When it comes
I curse the pain
Find no gifts in its
Being

How to transcend the
Physical when it is so
All-encompassing
Brutal

To say so
Is a
Beginning

I surprise myself when
I say to myself
Great suffering
Can be a
Great good

To suffer well
Is to enter it wholly
(Yes holy too)
Breathe it fully
Even though its
Acrid fumes
Smother hope

Good Friday

Suffering
Compassion
Immense Love
Letting Go

An awe that asks the world to
Stop for and instant to
Ponder the universality of its
Meaning

To allow the awareness that
Christ's suffering encompasses
All human suffering
That God's love is part of
All human love
That Christ's letting go is
Reflected in our
Learning to let go
That God's compassion and
Christ's compassion are
Gifts that allow us to
Begin to know
Human compassion

The rhythm of
Writing
Much like
The rhythm of
Walking
Begins to calm me

By writing
I can
Lean into my pain
Experience it more fully
Alleviate it a bit

I HATE feeling so
Weak and
Un-right
Dependent
Sad

I want to be
Strong assertive
Full of sparkle and
Enjoyment

Yet be in touch with
Sadness so
I can accept it and
Touch it in others

The urge to help is strong
It feels that since
I know pain
Can sometimes accept it
That I can then
Be there for
Someone else

I recognize that
Helping someone else is
Helping me

It's good therapy for me but
I think that's O.K.
It doesn't detract from it
Being good for the other
Rather it must enhance the goodness

The wounded healer perhaps but
I'm still in the process
I'm still finding my wounds
I'm still healing

Warm arms
Love
Music
Make the
Unbearable
Bearable

I dream
A lion with
His mane
Tied all around with
Bows

The dream
Spoke:
This means
Pain
Strengthened to
Love

I feel like a bear
Emerging from hibernation with
Tentative steps
Blinking at the brightness
Fur bristling in the breeze
Raising snout to
Sniff the promise of
Spring
Life

I am in awe of the
Body healing itself

On Monday I thought
I would never feel well again

It's Saturday
I do

5

Growth

With the diagnosis of
Terminal cancer
My life was
Coming apart so
I could stop
Having to hold
Everything together that
I thought I had to
Hold together.

It gave me
Permission to
Let things come apart.
I had nothing to
Lose now anyway.
It didn't matter.

At the same time,
Everything mattered as
It never had before.
Life acquired an
Urgency, an
Honesty, a
Realness
It never had before.

I began to come to
Terms with my own
Mortality -
Life as I know it -
Having a
Beginning and an
End.

I began to see
My life as
Something I could
Hold in my hands,
See its limitations in
Time and space, and
Know its
Potential for
Dynamic
Meaningful
Beauty.

Coming to terms with a
Terminal illness
Requires loosening some of the
Reins to the future

Things will happen
Decisions will be
Made without my
Contribution so
It's well to begin
Letting go now

When hope of survival
Begins to stir
I pick up the
Reins again but
Hold them a
Little more loosely
A little slack is a
Good thing

Cancer
Is an
Excuse a
Reason an
Opportunity a
Time a
Motivation an
Imperative for
Paying attention to
Self

I realize what is
Happening and
Try to pull away from
Allowing
Cancer to
Define
Who I am, to
Describe my
Outline, and to
Fill in the
Spaces within the
Lines

I'm so
Focused on the
Future and
Making informed
Choices that the
Present is
Buried beneath
Concerned pondering
Devoid of the
Richness
It must have

I try with
Awareness and
Being to be
Fully present in
This very moment

I want to know the
Reality of it
Feel the
Shape and
Weight of it

Knowing and
Accepting
This moment
I will be able to
Move into the
Next...and the
Next...and the
Next

Part of being present at
    this moment is to
Resist the urge to compare
    myself with
How I used to be

Simple tasks once done
    in a wink
Are no longer so

More extended ventures like
    packing for a trip
Are done in stages

Doing too much allows
    pain nausea fatigue to
Gather forces

Frustration is released
    in tears and
Giving in to tiredness

I counsel myself to be more
    careful next time and
Not expect as much

I remind myself that for the
    condition I am in
I'm not in such bad shape after all!

I'm looking for a
Definitive
"How to"
Even as I know
There is none to be given.

I'm in the process.
It's not a matter of answers.
Answers sound static.

I find plateaus of
Insight and
Developing beliefs,
Experiences along the way,

But they often
Change,
Grow restless,
Give way to new
Perceptions
Insights
Ideas.

What matters is
I am less afraid of the questions;
More open to where they lead.

In my forest of
Questions the
Path is
Cushioned with
Pine needles the
Scent is
Pungent and rich the
Tangled thickets are
Friendly
Overhead boughs become
Cathedral tracery the
Atmosphere is
Warm and moist
All elements
Invite
Participation

In the dream
I moved through
Mist-shrouded
Frost-covered
Forests and meadows

Men with guns were about

In a corner
(A corner not possible in reality but
Perfectly acceptable in the dream)
Near the end of the journey was a
Large tank-like weapon

I completely sensed and
Accepted the danger
Knew it was the right (a right)
Thing for me to do
Felt I could do it and
Would be all right in the process
No matter the outcome

I left others behind
Felt their pull but
Knew I had to go alone
Forces within - about - propelled me
I did not feel abandoned

I traversed vast
Distances with ease in a
Brief moment of time
Avoiding the gunmen by
Adjusting my pace or
Passing them unchallenged by
Emitting an aura that
Told them I was unarmed no threat

The journey ended in a
Small waiting room with
Several of us
Gathered in a corner
Ready for a rest yet
Refreshed from the
Accomplishment of the journey

Some sense of threat remained
Armed men at the door I think

A father told his son
"The important thing is that
You try your best to do it"
I think he meant to live

The hope of becoming is
Hard to hang on to when
I feel tenderness where
My liver is
(Has it metastasized to this
Most vulnerable organ?)
When my lower
Abdomen cramps
(Radiation damage?)
My thirst accelerates in
Prominent bursts
(Is my pancreas slowing
Production of insulin?)

I see these threats as
The gunmen in my dream
I see the parallels to
A journey I must in the
Final sense traverse alone
Support of medical knowledge and
Those I love can only go so far
The ultimate choices and
Doing are
Mine

Yet there are positive
Forces in the universe

Mysterious forces I can't explain
Yet I can accept as
Mysterious and positive
Helpful and loving to me
Not just to life in general
But to me individually as
A specific creation

Forces that really are
Helping me through the
Forest

Listen . . .
. . . .
. . . Listen
. .Listen . .

Listen to him
Listen to her
Listen to them

Listen . . .
Listen to myself
Hear the universe

The more I listen the
Fewer answers I know the
More questions I have

The more I listen the
More comfortable
I am with questions the
Fewer answers I need

The more I listen the
More is given the
More I hear

I don't actually tell
Too many people
I'm in therapy
Investing in emotional health

Admitting the need is a
Heady first step
Initial experience yields
Some pleasures and great pain

In spite of the pain and
The courage required
There's no turning back
Once doors begin to open

There's a lovely need to
Proceed to
Feel the textures of
Past and present in my hands

Much of it
Feels good the
"Aha" of sudden insight
Reaps progress and Joy

Really amazing is the
Grace that it is not too late
Indeed the time is right
To do it
To find me
To be me

Growing
Spiritually is
Humbling

I could point blame
Admit guilt that
I was wrong

More helpful is to
See it all as
Part of the process

Present
Discovery and
Openness

Arising from
Doubts constraints
Fears layered below that

Add substance goodness
Authenticity to the
Now

Right now
Therapy feels like
Clinging to a
Brick wall with my
Fingernails

Hellish oblivion
Yawns below
Unscalable heights
Stretch above
Yet I know
I'm in the right place
The process

My nails grow stronger

The weight of
Responsibility which
Often was preempted as
Youngest of five now
Depresses my soul
Constricts my breathing
Until Ed* offers a
Definition that
Sheds obligation
Frees my will:

Responsibility is the
Ability to respond

* therapist (editor's note)

I bend to
Embrace
Love
Accept the
Child within me

She rekindles
Delight
Long lost
I cherish the knowing

Her presence
Brightens my awareness
Breathes new
Life into my
Now

I can enjoy my
Self more now that
I don't spend so much time
Polishing and
Protecting my image and
Carefully keeping my
Emotions within
Neatly formed boundaries

The process of
Allowing my true
Self to emerge

Is often a
Soft quiet inner
Unfolding like a whisper

But sometimes it is
Loud and brassy and
Others want to cover their ears

I feel I have just
Emerged from a
Bout of the
Terrible Twos

I think my
Metaphorical
Kicking
Screaming
Egocentric
Rages are
Over

I've found enough
Me to
Go beyond
Me

I'm finding ways to
Accept parts of me
Give up parts of me
Forgive parts of me

In the dream
It was a gift of
A new cat

In reality
It is love
Acceptance
Wholeness

My anger
Becomes real
Legitimate

And with this
New status is
Dissipated

Seek diligently
Stride purposefully
Don't rest until
Every corner is
Swept clean

Open the windows
Let the strong breeze
Flow through
Purifying the very
Air we breathe

Resentment will
Live here
No Longer

Accepting
Forgiving
Reaching Out

Accepting
Forgiving
Reaching Out

Accepting
Forgiving
Reaching Out

Echoes in the
Cadence of my
Shuffle through
Drifting leaves

Becomes a
Melody in my
Mind Humming

But when is the
Rhythm finally
Learned

I try to
Reach for the
Reality of the
Moment:

See it,
Absorb it,
Incorporate it in a
Way that doesn't harm me.

Know when
I am caught.
Accept the
Caughtness.

Will myself into the
Struggle, the
Productive struggle of
New insight,

Resisting the
Conditioned way of
Turning it in on
Myself,

Now willing to
Look at my belief systems;
Deconstruct,
Reconstruct.

I'm learning to
Embrace all the
Shades of grey
Along the spectrum,

Take the opposite
Ends of the
Linear projection,
Bend them to a circle so

Opposites meet.
Extremes converge.
Yin and Yang dance.
All is acceptable.

Seems to me I have
Served enough time as a
Cancer patient

I've done my duty
Learned my lessons
(Promise to remember them)

Just let me off the
Hook now
Grant me parole

Stamp my papers
Say I'm released for
Good behavior

Let me wake up and
Find it was all a
Very bad dream

Therapy
Feels
On track again

Acceptance of
Where
I am in
My journey
Is there

Support
Guidance
Enthusiasm
Are there

The high tide of
Despair
Recedes
Revealing treasures in
Its wake that
Couldn't be without the
Trauma of the
Rolling waves

Hard-won gifts
Project from the firm sand
Respond to the warming rays
Glitter in their new life
Ripe for the gathering

Where does the balance come

Must one always keep count
Ears Eyes Mind Heart
Ever alert to signals to
Tally up the total of the
Primordial paradoxes so
Confidence doesn't become
Conceit so
Accomplishment doesn't become
Arrogance

Where am I
Really?

I'm incomplete
Let's hope so

I don't need to be perfect nor
Seek one right way to do things

I know I am not responsible for all but
I sometimes still feel it

I can often own my feelings and
Choose what to do with them

I accept more of myself all the time and
Enjoy the spillover of accepting others

I became more aware of
Who I am and why

I can sometimes investigate these whys
Without becoming overwhelmed with grief

I can pull back the curtain and
Begin to see the reality of backstage

I reenter my words to
Hone and shape them and
Reenter the experiences that
Formed them

The process is
By turns
Traumatic and
Therapeutic

I cringe at what I
Sometimes thought said wrote
Resist the temptation to modify

Feel I must leave it as it is
Accept it as it is
A valid expression of that time

I'm not writing to
Impress Inspire

Whatever
Validity
Impact
Significance

My writing may have
Stems from its
Committed attempt at
Realness

Sometimes it's
Damned good and
I relish the reading

Rereading rewriting reliving
Can be
Embarrassing
Painful
Joyful
Healing

Elizabeth asks with a
Lilt to her voice:
"Are you ready to come
Out of the closet with your writing?"

I've offered to read it at a
Summer church service so
Not only will my writing come out
But also my working with a therapist and
The expanding of my spirituality

I feel the wind
Catch the closet door
Hear it slam
Firmly behind me

Once out
There's no
Sliding back in

I have
Lost a
Dear person with my
Writing.

I miss her and
Grieve the loss.

She finds it
Unseemly for me to
Share the
Deep cut to the white bone.

She says
Let's not let this
Make a difference to our
Friendship.

But it does.
It is the stuff of which
Friendship is made.

We'll continue to meet but
Not in the same way.

Love comes round:

She wrote of my
Writing as a
"...gift of joy, a
celebration of living.
I was able to touch a
vast array of feelings-
both comfortable and
uncomfortable - safely,
and your work gave me the
courage to continue my
growth at a time when
I had decided I
really wasn't up to the challenge."

Her note,
Her courage,
Arrived to
Bolster my growth
Just as my
Resolve was waning.

We circle and dance.

My hope is that
Beyond the details and
Specifics of my writing
There is a universality that
Emerges
Meets others
Connects now and then with them
Engages them
Wherever they are on
Their journeys
And
We
Meet

Relying on my own
Strength is not enough.

Do I have?
Can I find?
Enough faith in
More than I am to
Let go and
Be?

I awoke,
Conscious of the word
Faith.

Not bolstered in any
Context,
It stands alone.
I don't quite know
What to make of it.

I accept it as a gift, an
Invitation, a
Suggestion to
Look for more;
Recognize it when it's there;
Allow it.

Faith in the universe?
In a god?
In myself?
In life?
In living life?

I stand alone more
Understand more the
Need to do so

The inevitability of
Ultimate
Separateness

(Ultimate
Unity
Wholeness?)

Will happen without
My willing
It in the end

Seeking it now
Learning its ways
Opening to it

Helps give voice to my
Self
Now

My view of the
World is
Changing

I see it in
My view of
Others

Acceptance
Rich regard for
Individuality

Celebrated within a
New awareness of our
Connections

I feel
Empowered
Enabled

Feel I can
Walk straight through
What isn't me and
Meet myself
Engage myself
Embrace myself

This awareness is a
Celebration
I want to
Sing it all

A small part
Holds back
Doesn't want to appear foolish
Is afraid to
Believe this
Could be me

Small part
You are allowed
Rest within the
Singing

I've known
All along that
I've been
Wedding
Conventional and
Unconventional
Treatment but
Didn't quite
Realize until now that
I have actually
Put together a
Something that has a label: a
Healthy holistic whole

Chemo
Radiation
Emotional therapy
Meditation
Imaging
Spiritual growth
T'ai Chi and now
Experimental biological
Response modifiers with
Some radioactive zap attached-
Monoclonal antibodies with
Iodine I-125

We're shopping for a VCR to
Add Cousin's
Laughter therapy with
Rented movies to our
Regime

Treating cancer
Holistically is
Treating life
Holistically

Gathering
Physical
Mental
Emotional
Spiritual
Forces into
One

It's exciting to
Sense a certain
Integration occurring.

Individual parts, once
Recognized,
Distinguished,
Alive in their own realms,

Become free to
Combine,
Flow,
Become a part of one another, a
Part of a greater whole.

If I can do this
(The this of cancer
The this of chemo)
I think I can do
Just about anything
I might decide to do

I am on a
Spiritual odyssey
Ideas feelings
Relationships abound
I want to
Taste them all
Absorb the
Influence of the ages
Sample the
Projections of the future
Marvel at the
Mysteries of birth and death
And the larger mystery of
Life itself in the
Magnitude of the universe

I count myself blessed to
Contemplate the questions

6

Loved Ones

He's the one
Who's there when
My spirits and
Courage flag

He's the one
I let my defenses
Down with and
Cry my tears of
Rage and pain

He's the one who
Will rub my back
Let me drink in the
Sweetness of warm
Comforting contact

He's the one
Who's been here
Twenty-five years
More than twenty-five but
Never closer than
Right now

When fireworks are
    no longer possible
It's a wonder to rediscover
    how tender a touch can be

It began when Terry said
"Show me where it hurts
Let me touch where it hurts"

His warm hands
Touched my
Sides back middle

This bloated
Scarred part of me that
I usually try to hide from
Him from me

His hands said
I accept this
Part of you

He entered into my
Pain and
Reality with me

Brought me
Soothing warming
Healing acceptance

Creating new
Connections with him
New connections within myself

His gentle caresses
Reduced tension
Relieved some pain

Invited me to
Relax into
Shared allowing

He clears the room so
She can scrub wax
Get cobwebs from corners
Cat toys from unders

He washes windows
Helps autumn glow in

As long as
Furniture must be
Shoved
Moved
Heaved
Back into
Place
Why not
Shove
Heave
It into
New places
Redesigning the room

Several new tries don't work
He digs his heels in

She begins to capitulate

He softens

They try the long couch under
Windows the
Windows
He just washed by the
Corners she just swept

Then all the rest
Find their places

They
And the room
Expand with
New Energy

Dear diary,
I forgot to
Tell you that
We rediscovered
Some time ago that
Fireworks are
Still possible

"I wish for you
Another love
When I am gone"

Their love
Won't replace
Ours

Theirs may
Feel
Freer
Easier

Theirs will
Draw nourishment
From our painful
Attempts at growth

I wish them abundance

I open the drawers of
My mind and
Explore the contents

I stroke the
Fine linen and
Soft cotton
Thin and
Satiny from age
I inhale the
Clean scent

They speak to me of
Simplicity
Orderliness
Refinement
Voices of my
Mother and
Grandmother

A lace collar in the
Bottom drawer
Adds a zest of
Elegance

I'm content to
Keep one piece
Replace the rest
Firmly close the
Drawers and
Return to me

Neighbor Nancy called this
Morning to say she would
Like to share tonight's
Casserole with us
I told her how wonderful that
Sounded but that
I would feel guilty
Accepting because
I am feeling well and
Quite capable of cooking
We agreed she would
Bring it anyway and
I could freeze it for later

When Martha brought my
Beloved tapioca last week
She threatened to take it
Back home because
I looked so healthy but
I wouldn't let her and
Practically ate it on the spot!

Once when Judy called while
I was in the hospital to
Ask if there was something
She could do
Terry told her tapioca
Was the only thing that
Sounded good to me
I don't think he realized
What he was asking
The egg separating the
Standing at the stove
Stirring constantly over
Low heat for ages
Oh my did it taste good and
Feel good as only tapioca can

It's time to write
Christmas cards
Again

I want to write the
Joy and love I feel
The sense of
Moving within a miracle

I want the words to
Shape the message both
Spare and precise
Round and full

Perhaps it is all too
Intense for a holiday note
Inappropriate among the
Exchanges of events

No what better
Time is there for
Celebrating spirit
Sharing life

In December
I realized
I might not see him* dance again

In June
I am flying to
New York to see him dance again

I hardly need a plane

*author's son Eric (editor's note)

What a wonderful
Time in New York

Close to Eric
Part of his life in person

Invited by 86 year-old
Gracious Madame Danilova* to

Bring my chair to the
Front of the studio with

Her and Freddy Franklin* to
Watch *Les Sylphides* rehearsal...to

Squeeze against the barre as
Waves of corps sylphs

Cascade downstage in
Powerful progression...to

Absorb the vision of Eric
Dancing dancing dancing

* late ballet dancers and teachers (editor's note)

I'll go with the
Doctor's Rx for
Increased hormones

Kristen* says
There's an abundance of
Hormones on campus

The place is so
Alive with them
Just breathing the air
Would be enough to supply
A therapeutic dose!

*author's daughter (editor's note)

Jo* and I talked trees on the phone-
Fragrance, shape, placement.

She reminded me that
Another wonderful thing about

Putting up the Christmas tree
Is that it is a perfect

Reason to once again
Rearrange the furniture!

*author's sister (editor's note)

Time is telescoping
It used to be
Make every day count

Now it's
Make every
Moment count

I must have
Six more
Months

February to
Rework my
Journal

March to see Jo in
California and
Kristen at home

April to go to the
Ocean with
Terry

May to see
Eric dance in
New York

June to see
Kristen come
Home again

For now I have to see
Yellow tulips
Bloom again

I can't count
That's only five
I still want six

If I really could
Choose how many
Would any number be enough

To spend
Meaningful time with
Friends, to

Deepen new
Relationships into
Friendships,

Means we need more days.

Why not stretch the
Arbitrary seven days, like
Modern composers do the scale.

A Schoenberg twelve-tone week
Sounds just about right!

I am full of feeling

Some of it bubbles
Some of it melts

Most of it gathers
Springs to the hearts of
Those I love

I hope they feel it
It's O.K. if they don't
I do

7

Appreciating Life

I mark my anniversaries and
Mark them well

They almost surprise me
Bring great pleasure and hope

A year ago mid-October
First symptoms appeared

A year ago tomorrow was
First surgery

A year ago the day before Thanksgiving
Was second surgery and

Diagnosis of cancer
Prognosis of a few weeks to a year to live

Here I am
Living

And living at a far different
Place from where I was a year ago

It's 11a.m. the
Monday after Thanksgiving
I just cleaned
Three rooms
Top to bottom

Last year on this day at
The eleventh hour as
I lay tethered to tubes
They gathered:
Dr. S.
Terry Kristen and Eric to
Tell me of the cancer
They already knew about

The news wiped out
My future in an
Agony of despair
Too painful to even
Begin to absorb

How good it feels to
Bend stretch reach
This day as I clean house

To remember the
Hard good work of the
Past year as my
Life my
Self
Learned to
Bend
Stretch
Reach in
New ways

My life-affirming barometer
Can be read in the
Level of my
Rearranging furniture activity.

Weeks ago we
Pushed, shoved, cajoled
Chests, bookcases, bed into
New configurations.

Energy born from
Post-chemo euphoria
Claimed radical changes in
Bedroom and
Living room.

Each room has acquired new
Spaciousness,
Congeniality,
Reflecting the developing,
Welcoming spaces within
Self.

Who would ever think that
Cleaning shelves
Organizing parts of my life
Could be so exhilarating!
To have the energy to do so
Astounds me

Looking at old sketch books
Resumes portfolio
Does not depress me as
Looking back sometimes does

Today it gives a positive boost to my
Rekindling of creative urges

I clear the debris and
Cobwebs from the
Room and from
Myself

The pure joy of
Puttering
Ironing a ribbon to
Wrap a wedding present

Puttering in my own kitchen
Grating apple in baked beans for
Tonight's block party

The ease the
Joy the
Contentment of
Puttering
Here...
...and...
there...
...and back again to me

The day after Christmas
I dashed out
It was still there
In my size
I bought it
The flowers and lace
In sweeping fullness
A dressing gown to
Nourish my
Romantic soul

To simply be alive
Is so delicious
I hug my knees
Like a nine-year-old

There are times when
I feel so vitalized so
Infused with the
Absolute joy and
Delight of
Living that
I want to
Lift off the ground and
Stride along the rooftops

I am less hesitant to
Reap joy when
I behold it

With hardly a second thought
I butter a slice of the loaf
Fresh from the oven and
Delight in its
Transient taste

With scarcely a twinge of guilt
I clip the daffodils as
They sway in their beds and
Transplant their glory to the
Kitchen table

I counted the
Little pleasures of the day
A bowl of cereal
Two showers
Noticing my nails needed attention
Having the energy to do them

Chemo is receding

I can't sleep
I sit on the deck
Watching hearing morning
    being born again

With careful listening
The mixed chorus of
Bird calls begins to
    sort itself out

Negative spaces of rich
Sky dominate between dark
Leaf and branch patterns
    in the woods

My senses stir in
Consort with the earth
A gentle way to begin
    a new day

Aware

I hadn't
Realized how
Open the
Woods had become

How much a
November
Woods

Until today
When I saw
Many many birds

Bare
Branches
Allow me to
Look
Deep

I stay up past
Midnight
Writing

Time seems too
Precious to
Spend it
Asleep

I love chocolate
Beethoven and
Writing

I especially love
Chocolate
Beethoven and
Writing at

Two in the
Morning when the
House
Is Mine

I'm more particular
Than ever about what
I wear

Above all I don't
Want a day to pass
Looking dowdy or
Middle-aged polyester!

I spend money on clothes as
My midriff expands and
Wish I could spend
Oodles!

I enjoy wearing what
I buy and
Put guilt on the
Back shelf with old hats

I want to hold life gently
To feel it fully
To treat it reverently

Andre Watts is fully present
To every note of the
Beethoven concerto

Beethoven
Brings strength

Love courage
Shine through his
Suffering

Emerge on an
Ethereal plain with

Humankind and
Godlove
Awakened

So tender so
Loving in
All its
Magnificence

Made more so by so
Powerful and tormented
A man creating
Music which at
Times is
Exquisitely delicate

Beethoven's Ninth
Is an intravenous
Shot to the soul
That asks
Why do I
Waste my Self with
Anger and despair when
Beauty and
Love
Are there for the
Sensing

It's my beloved
Mozart's
Birthday
Today
We're only a day apart

I listen to
Absorb his
Requiem and
Mourn for the
Suffering of his last days

The "Sanctus"
Swells with
Measured dignity
Ends abruptly
Too soon
As his life did

I wonder which
Bar is his last
Which notes his
Student completed

Was he really so
Haunted
Guilt ridden by the
Imposing figure of
His father as the
Movie would have us believe

Dear Amadeus
I am so grateful
I don't have to
Envision
Don't have to hear
A world without your genius

I can't die yet
There is
Too much
Music to
Hear

I am 49 today

A new age
Like a new year
Sounds strange at first
Needs some wiggling into
Until the corners fit

I do like the
Sound of it though
Old enough to
Feel life but
Not so old

Kristen* said it's a
Number she's always liked
Because it's 7 X 7 and
She likes 7's

Which reminds me
That ever since
I was a child I
Have known 7 is
My lucky number

49 has a nice
Rounding off essence
To it that
Allows for
Thinking about endings

And thus beginnings

* Author's daughter (editor's note)

The City*
Awakes
All parts of me
Allows
All parts of me

In perfect paradox the
Impressive crush of people both
Mandates separateness and
Engenders acceptance

Perhaps the push to
Be an individual in
Order to survive the
Demands the city makes

Allows people to
Meet as individuals
Aware of their own edge
Making allowance for others

*New York City (editor's note)

At MOMA *

I sit and drink it in
The cool still waters in
Dark shades with a
Glint of pink
Soon give way to a
Subdued riot of hues
Expertly layered to
Create atmosphere

I can plumb the depths and
Can't believe it's oil paint
It sure looks like pastels but
Surely couldn't be on
Such a mammoth scale

My eyes caress the canvas
Move from light to dark and
Back again
I feel the
Serenity and the
Excitement that
Occupy the same space and
Wonder at the genius that
Fills the room

Thank you
Monet for your
Water Lilies

* Museum of Modern Art, New York City (editor's note)

St. Augustine Beach

The rounded birds
Brown above
White below
Skimmed back and
Forth with the
Roll of the waves
Their sturdy bodies
Multiplied by sleek
Reflection in the
Shining sand

Jung finds
Wholeness in groups of
Four and ten but
My artist's eye
Celebrates the esthetic and
Dynamic impact of three and five
The lack of symmetry
Paradoxically providing
Visual balance

To satisfy both
Psychology and art
I could paint four birds but
Group two so close together they
Function as one visual element
An even number for the
Therapist to count and the
Stability of the
Triangle of three with
Essential focal point for the
Artist to hang his theory on

When the impressive
String of pelicans
Soared over in
Follow-the-leader
Swoops of wing
There was not time for
Abstract analysis
It was like counting
Cars in fast-moving
Freight train
Seventeen

Low tide is my
Favorite time for
Walking

The long sandbar is exposed
I walk between crashing waves and
Still lagoon alive with birds

Bathing
Fishing
Eating

The rhythm of the
Walking the
Music of the waves

Mesmerize me
I continue almost
Further than energy allows

After walking an
Hour and half this
Morning

I folded into
Three hours of deep
Sea-air drugged sleep

Hips knees ankles are
Sore from so much exercise on
Uneven sand but

How good to feel pain
Emanating from a
Healthy source

Full of pleasure
Free from
Fear

The sun rose with a pop
Eliciting a soft involuntary gasp from me
As we shivered on the pier
Awaiting our star's red hot
Annunciation of a new day

Try as I may
I couldn't fit Earth's
Rotation motion notion into any
Convincing configuration

The best I could do was
Think about it having
Already visited England

It felt like it had
Traversed the Atlantic to
Us rather than our
Rolling into its view

To walk the
Ocean's edge is to
Trod along the
Soul of the earth in
Measure with the
Pulse of the Universe

Green grass
Gives way to
Color-laden hills
Beyond red of
Dogwood below

Grey sky
Hangs low over
Crest of a ridge
Slice of orange sky
Radiates below

I am pulled
Pulled into
Beauty
Pulled out of the
Ordinary

I am alone
Unleashed from
Family
Friends
Doctors
Therapy

Wholeness
Sings from the hills
Reaches out to
Embrace me

I sink into the
Love the
Potential the
Healing that is
Here
Bring my Self to it

-Le Shan Healing Seminar

The retreat house
Was for me a
May Sarton house:

New England
Rural
Full of surprises

I longed to
Catch a glimpse of her
Garden flower bouquet as
I rounded a corner on
Worn-smooth creaky floor

The bay window
(filled with sun when
storm clouds parted)
Begged for a chair
Right there

I was tempted to
Rearrange the room
So the sun's
Warmth and hope
Would not be
Lost

I had a hint
Last year

Now it's evident:

The desperate grasping of a
Last Christmas has faded.

It's this Christmas.
It's now.

Be in the snowfall.
Catch flakes on my tongue as
They fall fast and thick.

I seek
Pleasure in the
Potential of
Now, the
Beauty of this day,
Released from
Preoccupation with
Cancer and
Death

Today it happened
Although the red are still in bud and the
White ones are widely open already

Today my
Yellow tulip
Bloomed its
Spring for
Me

Has your driveway
Been this glorious
Every spring Barbara

Have you really always
Had such shades of
Red orange pink

Has the late afternoon sun
Always set your periwinkle
Aglow in Alpine silver

I imagine your garden is the same
And the spring is the same
It's me who is different

A glorious morn

Blue sky
White clouds
Brisk air

Dvorak's *New World Symphony*

I feel the dawn of
My own new world

8

Meditation & Visualization

Meditation
One infinitesimal speck
Perceived in my vision
Is a link to the
Whole of the universe

Five days of chemo and
Five days of meditation
Leave me intimately
Involved with myself on
A cellular level

I am aware of
Mental and spiritual
Communication within my body

I can consciously recognize
Emotional stress that drains
My positive resources and then
Quite sensibly I can shut it down

I can applaud a rise in
Spirits and channel
Some of that enthusiasm to
Bolster a flagging organ

I can allow my whole to
Just settle and give it
Time to discover itself
Accept where it is

Then physically
Mentally
Emotionally
Spiritually
My Self
Can proceed along the
Path that is right for me

Tomorrow I find out
Bone marrow results

I feel caught

Caught between surgery to
Remove my spleen if
It's responsible for
Low platelet counts

Beginning the harsher chemo
Regimen of Adriamycin or

Allowing the disease to
Take its course

In my depression
I forget to remember
Healing

I seek solace in
Meditating

The cool waters of
Peace and love
Ease the throbbing
Dis-ease and
Bring my Self
Together again

My music therapy
Feels powerful.

Listening only
Begins with my ears.
Head and heart
Listen, too, but
Then they always
Have when genuine,
Active listening is
Involved.

The difference
Now is that
All my body is
Experiencing the
Music.

I primarily receive it
Through my middle in
Sounds emotions vibrations.
It soothes or excites,
Expands or contracts
Viscera, muscle, blood vessels,
Organs, glands, pancreas.

At concerts
I let my body
Sprawl and open to
Catch as many
Elusive notes as possible.

Some tapes are so much
A part of me now that
Different movements
Elicit specific responses.

I sometimes
Follow
Morning meditation
Or extend it with
Mozart.

Laudate Dominum from a
Vesper cycle, with
Kiri Te Kanawa's
"Amens" soaring above the
Grounded chorus,
Awakes all parts of me to the
Wonder of life in
Every inch and fiber of
My being.

His motet,
Ave Verum Corpus,
Floods my
Pancreas with
Love acceptance hope;
Delivers it from
Role of victim.

I use *Exsultate, Jubilate*,
Especially the
"Gloria," to
Stimulate my bone marrow,
Calling it to
Produce
Red cells white cells platelets.

I bid my pancreas
"Listen" to the last movement of
Mahler's Second Symphony
It did

It felt the vibrations the
Life-affirming
Swell of theme and
Answering French Horns

Usual imaging of
Malignant cells being
Swept away was
Replaced by just
Strong infusions of healing

All of me
Experienced the
Music in a
Realm beyond
Hearing and
Intellect

When the pain
Attacks with
Brutal force the
Discipline of
Meditation
Deserts me

I reach for the
Percocet first
Then return to
Mental powers to
Help calm me

Enhancing the
Effectiveness of the
Prescription and
Making the passage of
Time tolerable until it
Begins to take hold

T'ai Chi
Feels
Beautiful

Even as
Muscles
Rebel at

Enforced
Discipline

Steps
Positions
Flow into

Fluid
Connections

Mind
Focused on
Remembering

Morning meditation
Followed by T'ai Chi
Leaves me
Moving freely
Breathing fully
Cleansed
Opened
Invigorated

All parts of me
Becoming

Meditation was once a
Duty to perform in
Anticipation of benefits

Now it is both a
Necessity and a
Luxury

I need it every morning
Look forward to its
Velvet welcome

Golden and rare is the
Moment in meditation when
All that is in me can become
Consciously present to that
Moment

Expanding
All that I am to fill it

Filling it to overflowing yet
Neither dipping back into the
Moment just passed nor
Anticipating the
Beat of the
Next

I meditate
The clock peals ten

The strikes say
My time has come
My time is now

I gather it all
Into myself and
Run with the wind

I settle in quiet as
Dew on
Morning blade

Reflecting all about
In one
Shining droplet

My time is now
To know to love
To be

I gather it all
Within me
Hold it close

Let it go
Marvel that I
Can know it

Often
When I return to the
Reality of my room after
Meditating

She's sitting there
On the edge of the bed
Looking pleased

She likes it
She senses I am more
Cat-like when I meditate

9

Insights and Inspiration

Inspiration in the
Spiritual and
Artistic sense
Mirrors the physical
Meaning of the word:

An inrushing of
Fresh air and
Life

It doesn't
Die with
Expiration

On the day of my diagnosis
You saw a beautiful rainbow in
Your rear-view mirror and
Called it my rainbow
Knew I would be all right

When you heard the report
Denial came to your defense
You refused to believe the
Rainbow betrayed you and
You pray for a miracle

My wish for you is an
Expanded view with the
Unfolding of the miracle that
Even though I have cancer in
Some ways I am
More all right than ever

I would gladly
Give back the cancer if
I could but

I want to
Keep all it
Has taught me

What helps most and
Brings me some
Degree of peace
Is to view what's
Happening in the
Larger context of
All that is happening

Somehow it makes it
Belong to a sphere of
Meaning
Rather than some
Isolated cruel event

I don't know who
Developed the concept nor
How it evolved or

Why I'm just now
Becoming aware of it but
It's satisfying to view
Past
Present and
Future as one

It makes me a
Part of all that
Has been
Is and
Will be

Not only is
My history there
To be remembered but
All of history lies within
A continuum of the
Universe within my
Soul stretching
Backward
Forward and
Non-ward
Further than
One can see or
Imagine

Interiors
I rearrange the
Furnishings in my
Body in my
Mind in my
House

Novel combinations
Some discarding
New acquisitions
Create my own style
Redefining me

To draw again
Is to feel the
Splendor of creating

When I am
Creating all parts of
Me are alive

Once alive the
Parts become aware of
One another and harmony follows

Creating creates a
Superb environment for
Healing

A portion of
Grace comes
Settles
Allows

I open
Release
Love

Allow
Imperfections
Let go of
Needing to do so
Much myself

Allowing
Seeps in
I float

Feel peace

Tight fear loosens

The
Call the
Presence the
Choice is there

I seek the
Courage the
Way the
Permission from
Self to
Receive

Profound acceptance of a
Kind I've never known
Is given me

I can settle at the bottom
Allow that I cannot
Handle all of life myself

A power that is
More than I am
Is there for me

Within me

Can come through me

To help
Embrace
All of
Life

I settle quietly
Feel for the
Still pool within me
Reach for the power beyond me
That in remembered love
Will now collect my
Splintered self in
Reassembled
Comfort
Strength
Love
Recalling my
Spirit to
Rejoice in the
Goodness of the
Moment

Feet firmly planted in my
Unitarian
Liberal growing, with
Openness its seed,
I am freed to
Reach for the
High flowering
Branches of
Spirit

Why do I have
Such a hard time
With the word
God

I embrace the concept

The reality embraces me

Yet the proper name God
The pronoun He
Throw up barriers of
Remoteness

I'll forgo the words

Open to the part
Within
Without
That allows brokenness
Seeks wholeness

The part that is
More than I am

If there is a
Living God, a
Spirit that
Cares about my
Everyday living,
He must be an
Avid reader, or
Perhaps a
Librarian.

How else
Could
Just the
Book I
Need
So often
Come to me?

I move within a
Different dimension
An added dimension
(I'm not sure which
It doesn't matter
I can feel it
Don't have to
Dissect it
Intellectually)

I'm out of schedule of
Morning meditation and
Imaging but feel
Awareness of
Body mind spirit soul
The presence of what
I call God
Moving within me

A loving healing pulse
Circulates throughout me
Touching healing making aware
Then flows to all around me

I like discovering
God within me at a
Peaceful time when I feel
I am not clutching at straws

Then I can know
His presence when
I am sick in pain
Unable to function
More confident to
Open to it in the
Dark valleys having
Known it on the
Sunny peaks

Blessings knowing openness
New awareness connections
Burst upon me
Bringing unaccountable love
Affirming of Self
Giving up of Self

It's not just a
Theoretical observation of
Mankind but an
Actual event happening to an
Individual - and
It's me

Why
How
It's almost more than I can absorb

Dear God
Teach me to open to
Your gifts of
Love trust giving
That they may
Flow through me to
Others...and
I may know them
More richly in
My own heart
Along the way

I've never really understood the
Essence of the Holy Spirit but
At the risk of sounding
Sacrilegious (irreligious?)
I feel it move within me

I feel it because
I feel my spirit and
All spirits are holy

I feel it swirl
Delightedly within me as at the
Same time it trails off into the
Universe and encompasses
All

I hear it in the oboe in
Beethoven's Ninth
I see it in the ballerina's
Elegantly placed toe
I feel it in Van Gogh's
Poppy Fields

The wonder of it astounds me

My cells are different
My senses are different
My very being is changing

I shed heavy cloaks of
Assumed identity and
Quiver at the rapturous
Emergence of Self

My being transcends
This place this time
Yet is ever a part of it
As it is of the universe

I am here
I am me
It is good

I feel wrapped
Loved
As if a magnificent
Bird of the universe
Settles his wings about me

I swim in the
Warm accepting
Waters of
Amniotic fluid with
Amphibian flips of
Delight in
Remembered
Evolution of Self
Embraced in
Godlove

To reduce mystery to
Ordinary words
To attempt to describe spirit
Eludes me

I'm stuck with trying to
Tell about my
Eyebrow as a conduit for
Spiritual awareness

Seems more at home in a
Byzantine mosaic
Highlighted against the flat
Richness of blue with golden stars

Than it does in a
Rational
Twentieth century
Journal

My
Growing
Changing
Perception of
Me and of the
Universe
Affects the
Very air
I breathe

I celebrate the
Change within me that
Affects the
Universe

I anticipate my
Change in
Perception
Manifesting in
Thought
Word
Action
Impacting on me
Others

Profiting the
Universe

The
Universe is
User
Friendly

Transcendence

I could see beyond
Now
I could feel beyond
Sensing
I could be beyond
Here

I traveled beyond
All I know
All I feel
All I am

On a trajectory beyond this
Sphere

I found
Love
Wholeness
Oneness that

Asked:
"How could you
Imagine I didn't exist?"

"How could
Anything
Mean anything
Without me?"

I am not alone

Beyond the intellect,
In a corner of the soul where
Intuitive glimpses of
More than we are,
Occasionally,
Repeatedly,
Blink their presence,

There
Can we
Nod
Yes

Within any dimensions
Life can be lived.
As physical limitations limit,
Spiritual expansion expands.

Thoughts of
Cancer
Pain
Body function
Recede as

Chemo
Monoclonal antibody
Treatments
Cease,

Their
Capacity
Reached

Healing
Meditation
Continues,

Overdosing not a
Concern of
Love.

My eyes have a different look
I hear it from people who try to
Define the difference then say
"You look the best I've
Seen you in a long time"

My body has a different feel
Even on mornings when sleep is
Hard to push away

My mind collects different insights
I chuckle at sudden
Recognition of whats and whys

My soul has a different grounding
Rocked in loving
Awareness

Irrepressible
Surge of
Joy

Awakes
Declares
Sings

Life
Is a
Gift

I feel a
Cosmic beam
Shooting
Straight for the
Stars

To play among the stars,
To hear the chorus of the universe, is
To open my Self to
More than I am

The ocean
Roars its paradox

It says
I am alone

It says
I am part of all

It weds patient
Persistence

With fleeting
Dynamics

Individual waves
Exist for a moment

As a whole it has
Existed forever

I walk the ocean edge
Explore my mind edge

Try to find myself in the
Cycle of living and dying

Attempt to feel a comfortable
Stride within the paradox of

Welcoming connections
Abiding with
Necessary separations

The unrelenting ocean
Repeats with each
Breaking wave:
"Celebrate the mystery"
"Celebrate the mystery"

About the author

Suzanne Elaine Teagle Lindemer was born and raised in Crown Point, Indiana. She earned her undergraduate degree from Ball State University, her Master of Arts in Education from The University of Florida, and worked professionally as an elementary school teacher. She and her husband Terrence Lindemer settled in Oak Ridge, Tennessee, in the late 1960s to raise their two children, Kristen and Eric. As a writer, Suzanne served as *Lifestyles* editor for The *Oak Ridger*, and documented her experiences of living with cancer through journaling. A lifelong lover of music, she played piano and recorder. She was also an artist who specialized in painting, drawing, and woodblock printing. Suzanne passed on October 4, 1990 from pancreatic cancer. Her spirit lives on through her writing, her artwork, and in the hearts of those who love her.

To order additional copies of this book, including the e-book version, visit:

About the editor

Eric Brian Lindemer (son of the author) was born in Oak Ridge, TN and has worked in the performing and healing arts. He studied at the School of American Ballet in New York City and danced professionally with American Ballet Theatre, Boston Ballet, and Les Grands Ballets Canadiens. Also a Certified Massage Therapist, Eric has taught movement and healing arts at institutions throughout the U.S. including Boston University, Harvard University, The Massachusetts Department of Developmental Disabilities, Brigham and Women's Hospital, and the Sedona Creative Life Center. His current focus is teaching meditation, massage, and energy healing for personal and professional enrichment.

For information on Eric's live events, products, and on-line offerings visit:

~~www.templeofthelight.net~~

www, theawakeninglight .com

978-501-4180

universallight333 @ gmail. com

263

Made in the USA
Lexington, KY
23 May 2018